Counting from 1 to 20

Count 1 to 20

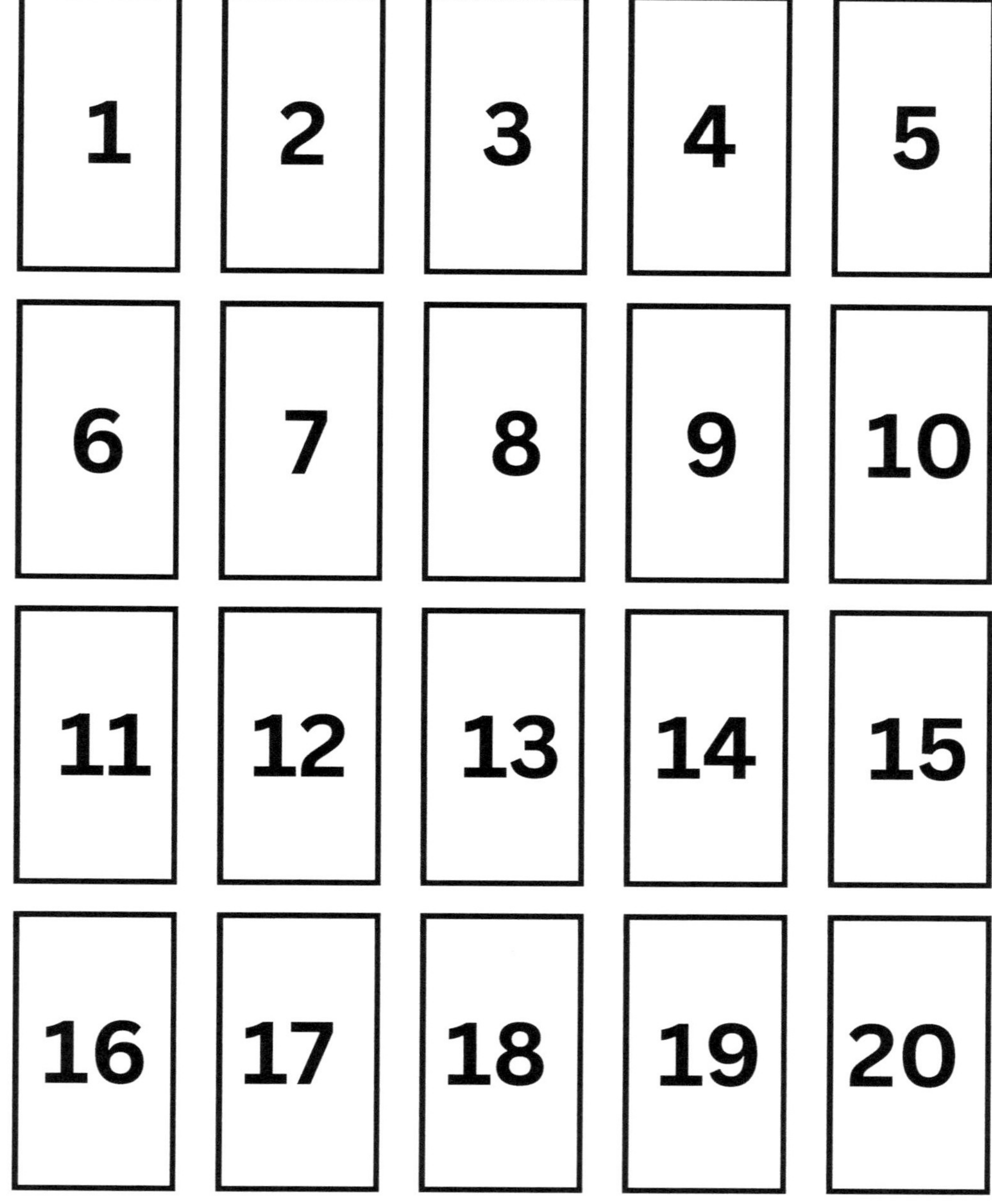

Number names 1 to 20

1	=	One
2	=	Two
3	=	Three
4	=	Four
5	=	Five
6	=	Six
7	=	Seven
8	=	Eight
9	=	Nine
10	=	Ten
11	=	Eleven
12	=	Twelve
13	=	Thirteen
14	=	Fourteen
15	=	Fifteen
16	=	Sixteen
17	=	Seventeen
18	=	Eighteen
19	=	Nineteen
20	=	Twenty

Trace

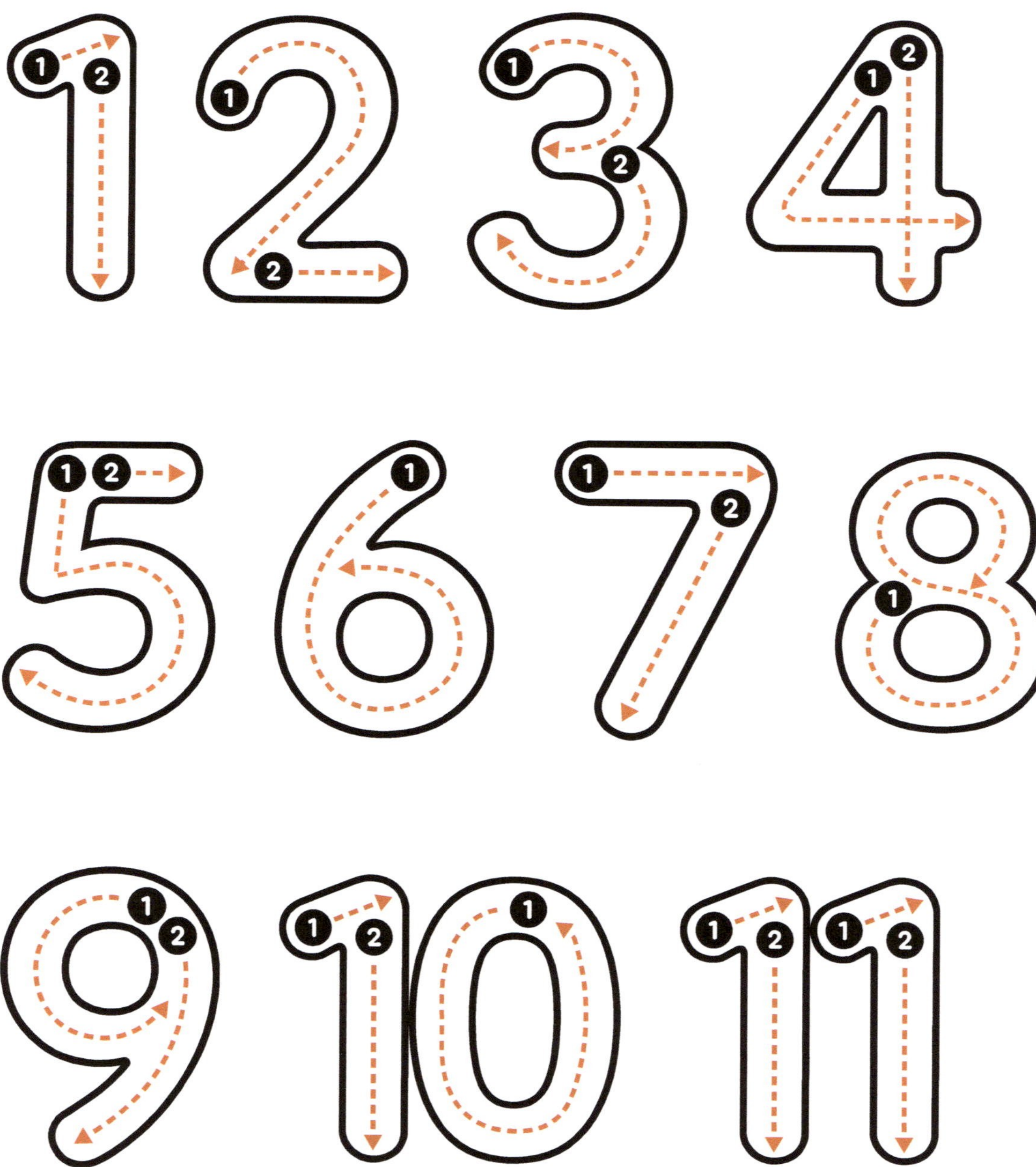

Trace

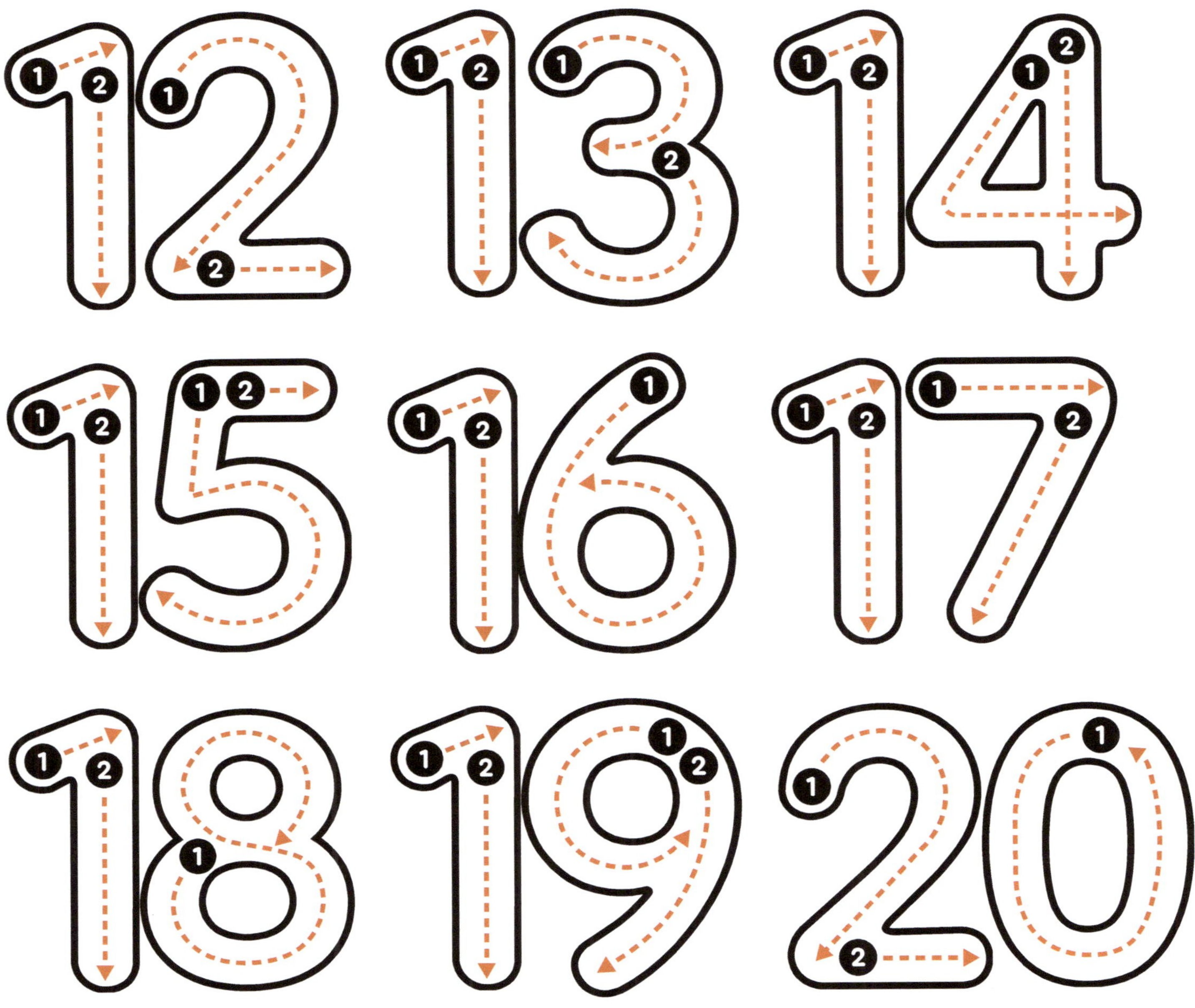

Number Zero

Zero is like the invisible ninja of numbers, sneaking in when there's nada to count or measure.

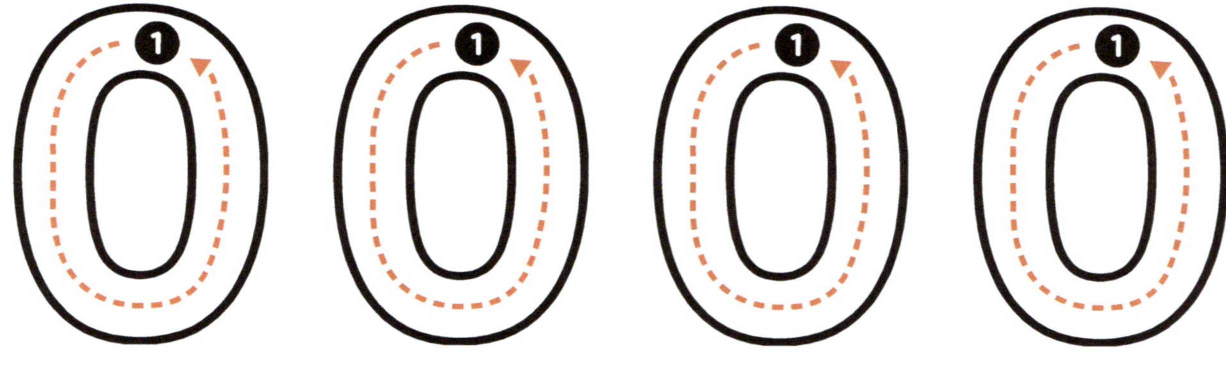

Count and match the number of fingers

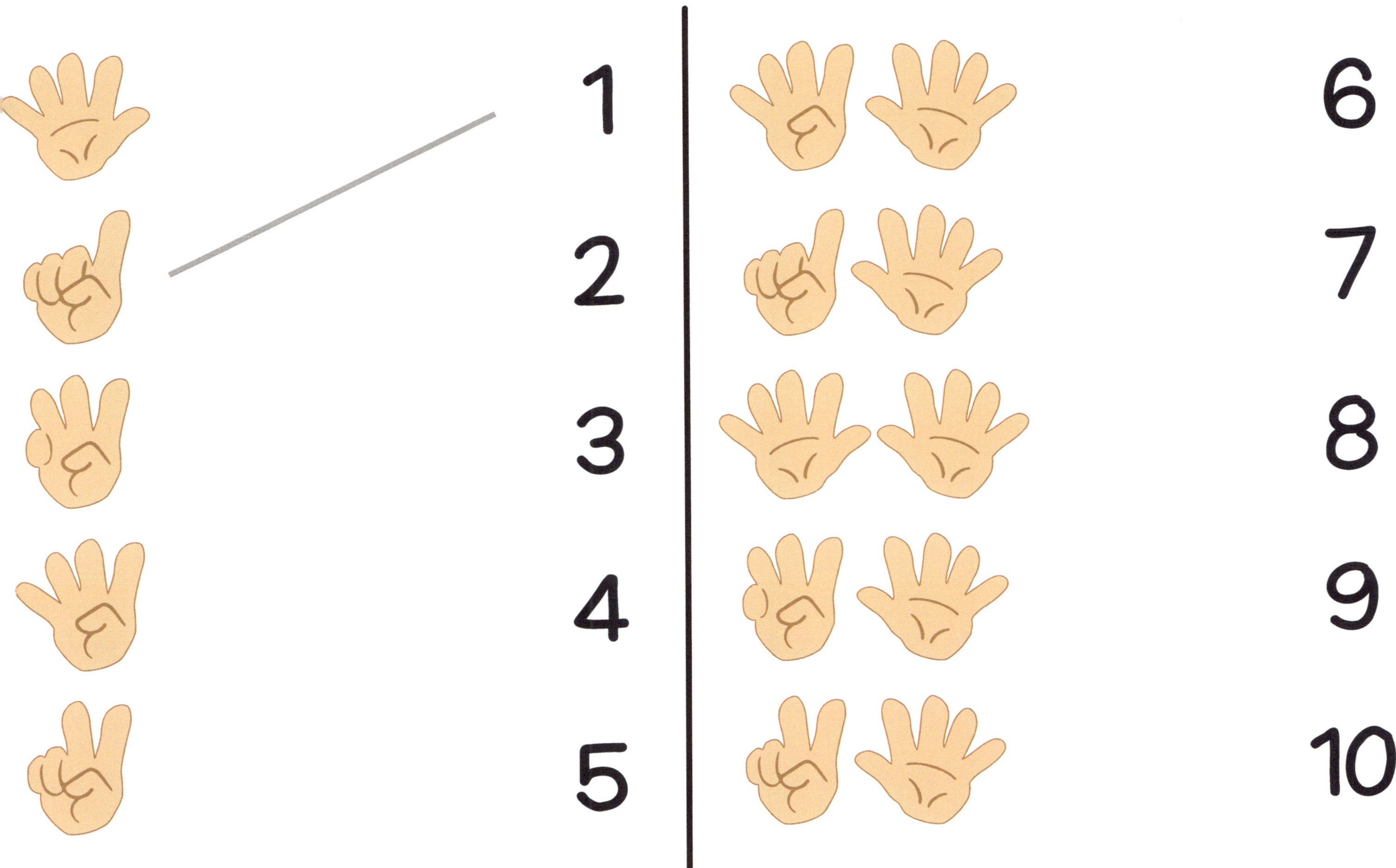

Count and match with correct number

1

2

3

4

5

Count and match with correct number

6

7

8

9

10

Count and match with correct number

11

12

13

14

15

Count and match with correct number

16

17

18

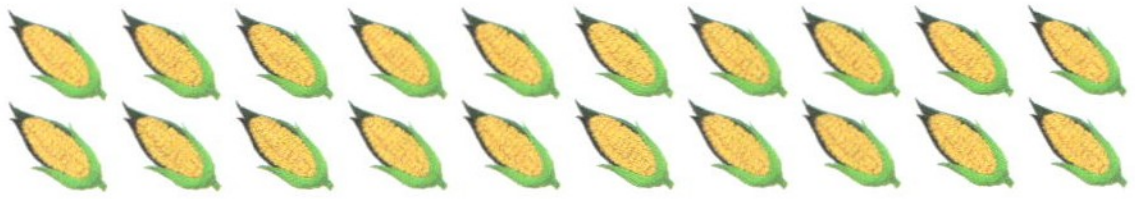

19

20

Fill in the missing numbers

Draw a line between numbers and their words

Draw a line between numbers and their words

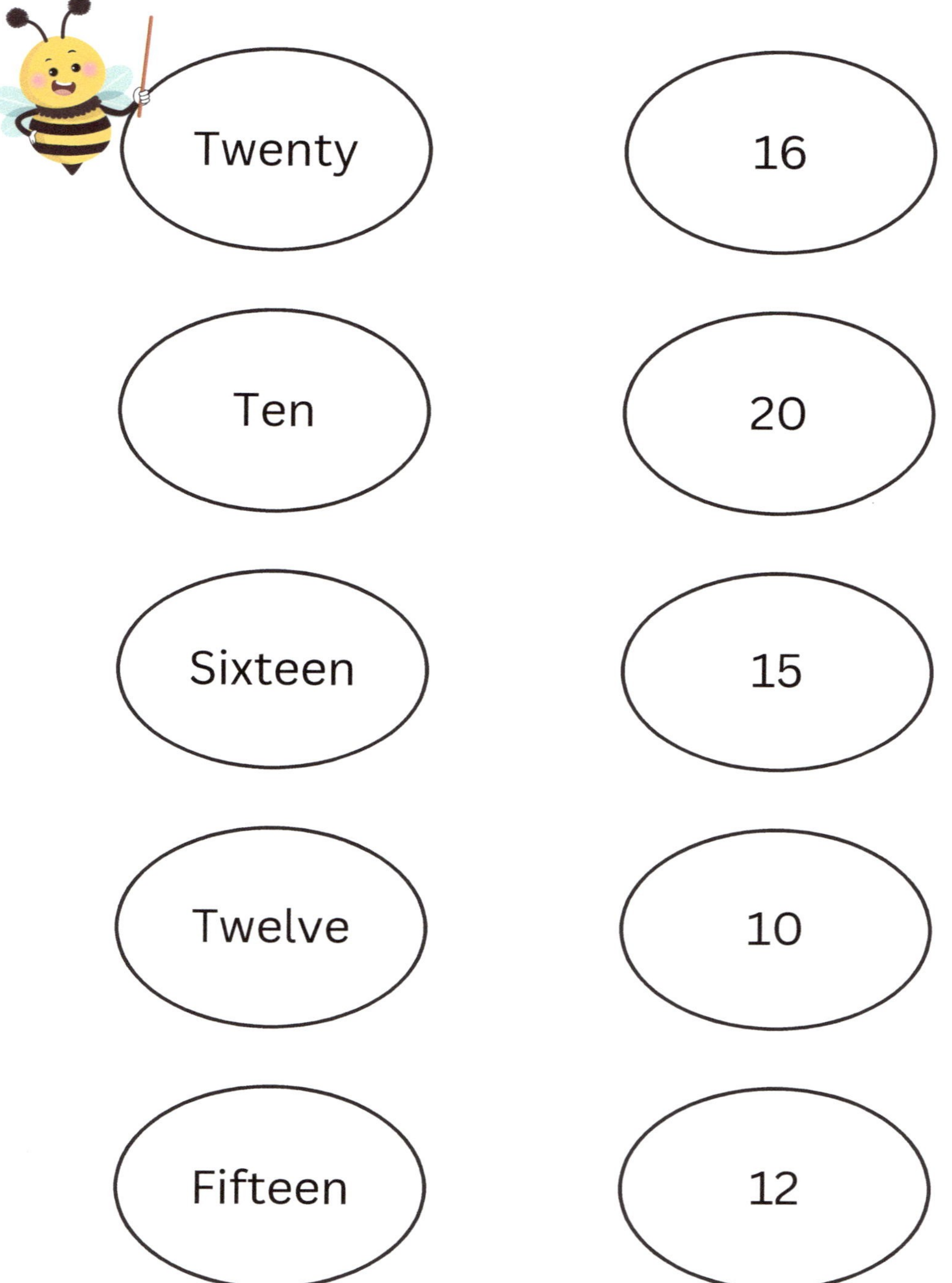

Draw a line between numbers and their words

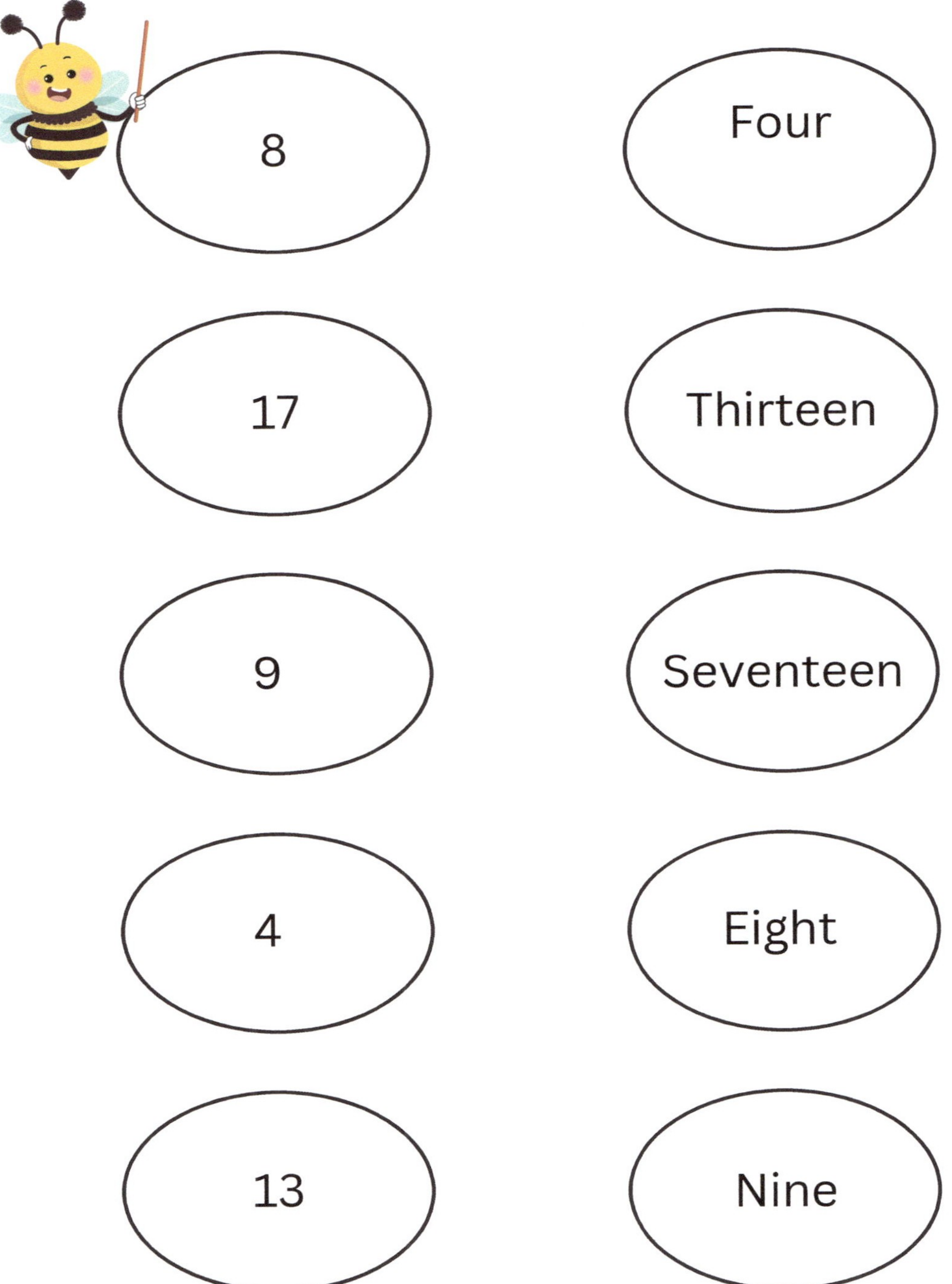

Count and write the number of objects

Count and write the number of objects

____

____

____

Count and write the number of objects

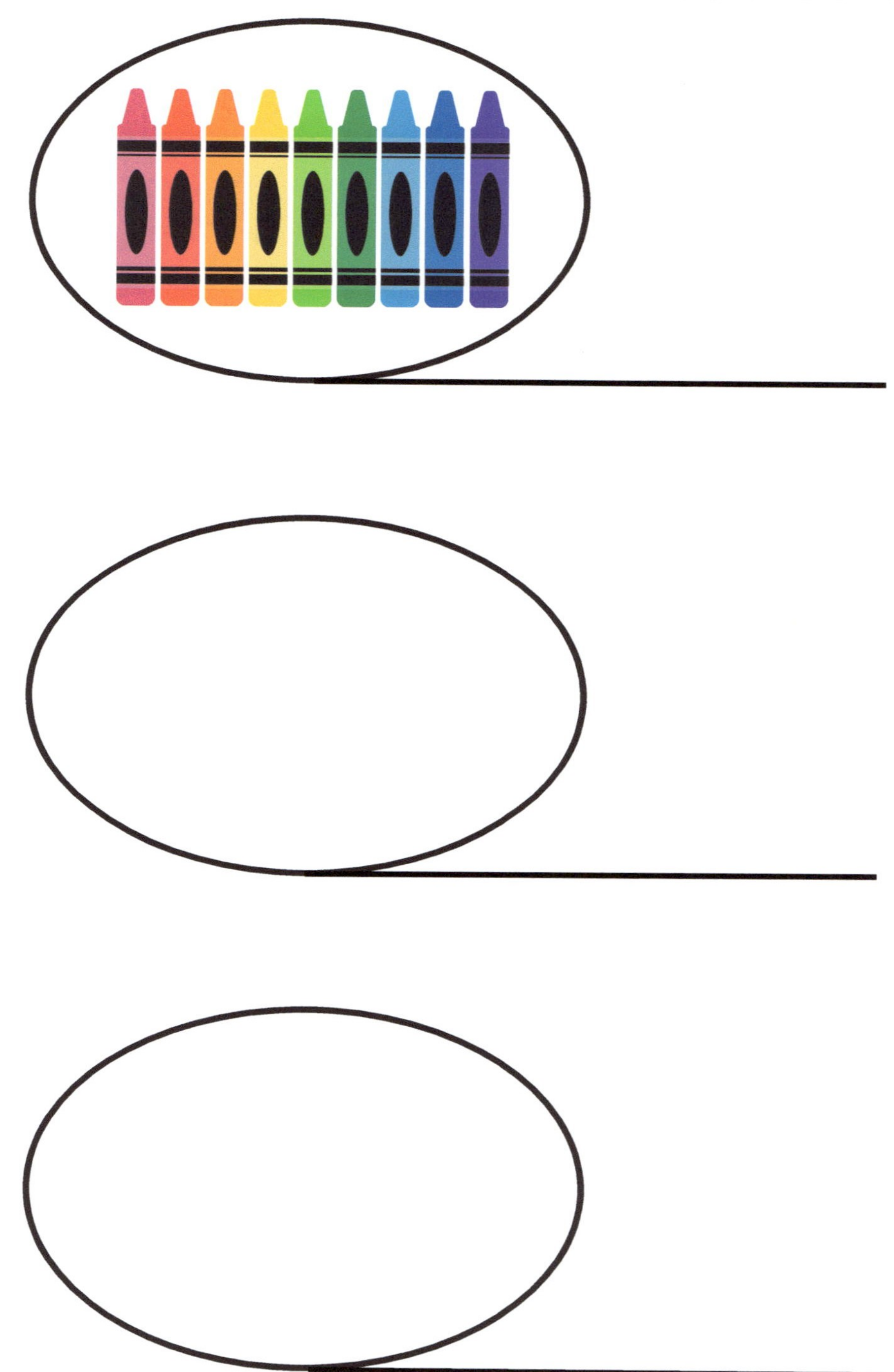

What number comes before

What number comes before

What number comes after

What number comes after

Ten Frame

Fill in the number for each frame

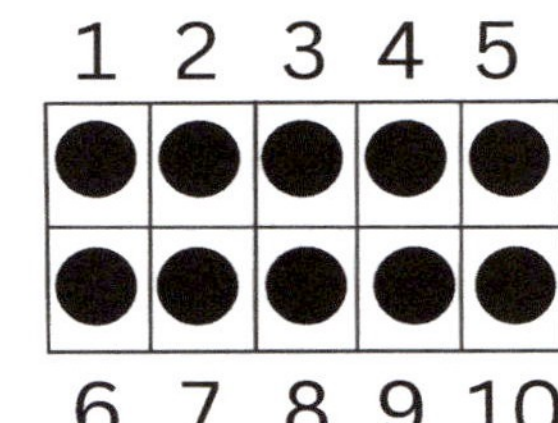

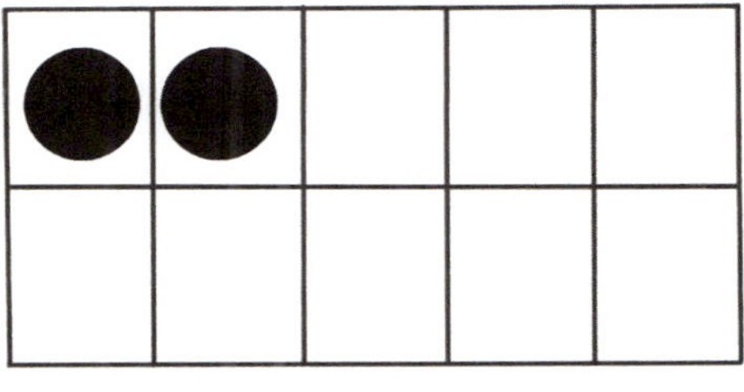

2

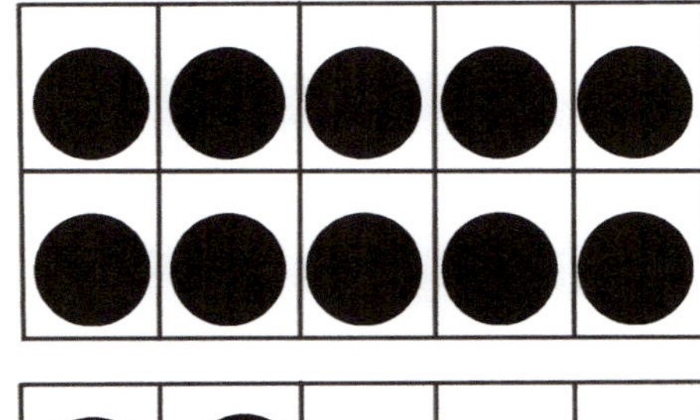

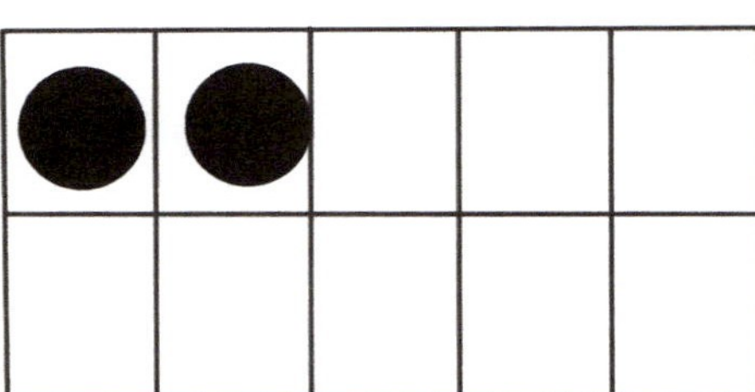

12

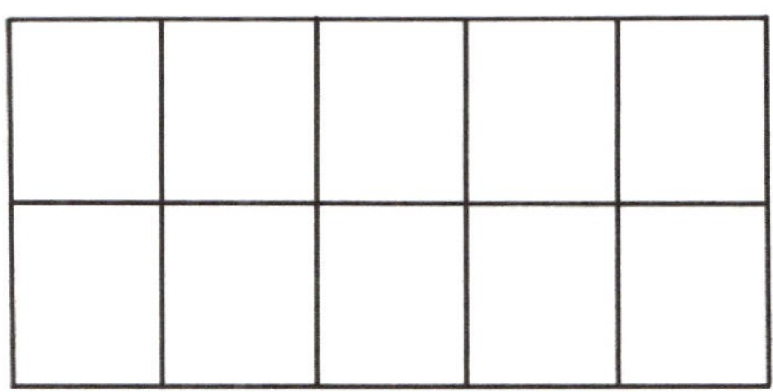

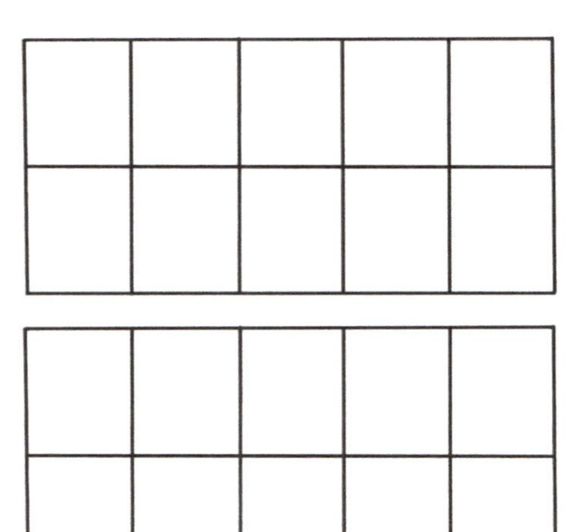

Number Line 

Use the number line to
complete the problems

Addition

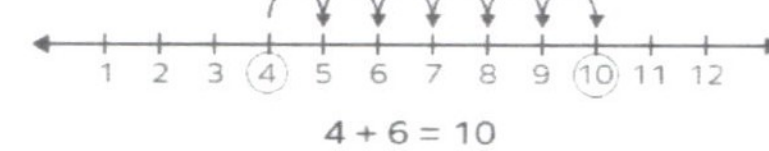

| 6 | + | 2 | = | | |

1 2 3 4 5 6 7 8 9 10

| | + | | = | | |

1 2 3 4 5 6 7 8 9 10

| | + | | = | | |

1 2 3 4 5 6 7 8 9 10

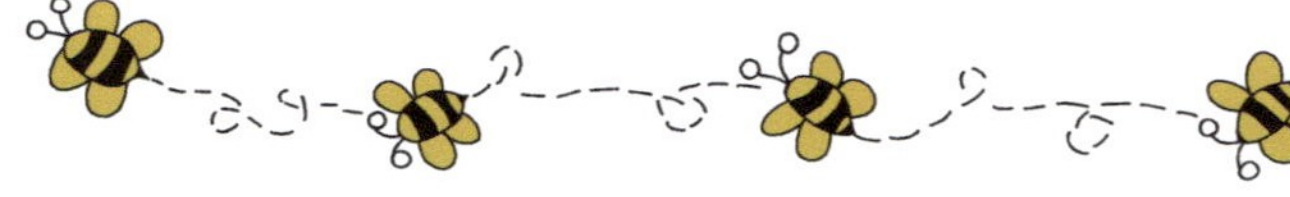

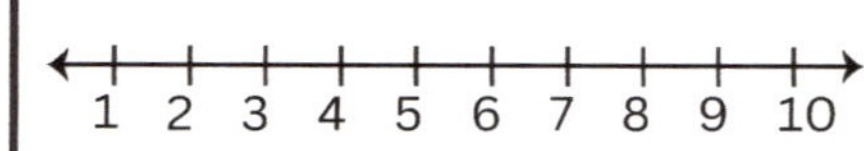

Subtraction

| 5 | - | 3 | = | | |

1 2 3 4 5 6 7 8 9 10

| | - | | = | | |

1 2 3 4 5 6 7 8 9 10

| | - | | = | | |

1 2 3 4 5 6 7 8 9 10

Place Value

Count the blocks, then complete blank spaces

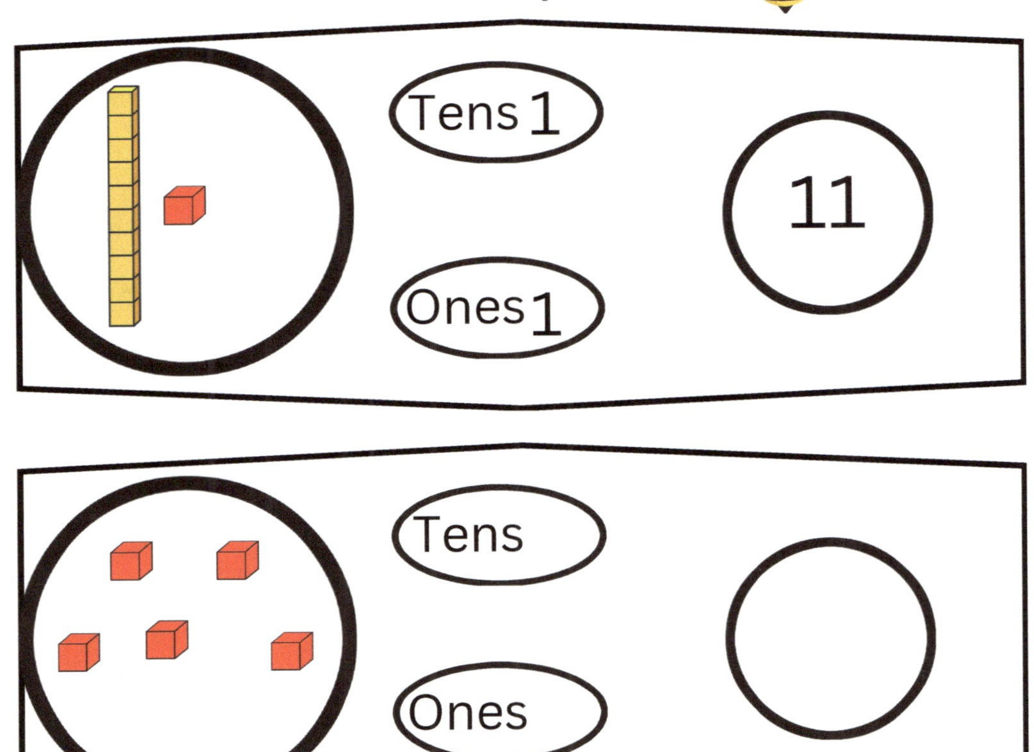

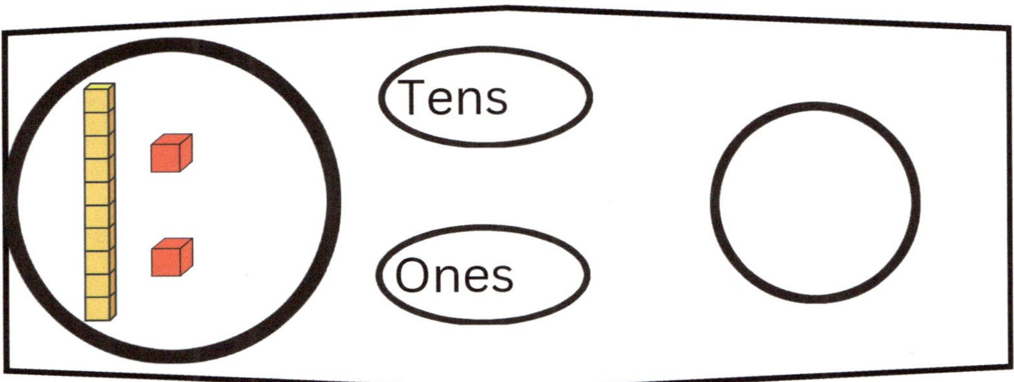

Place Value

Count the blocks, then complete blank spaces 🐝

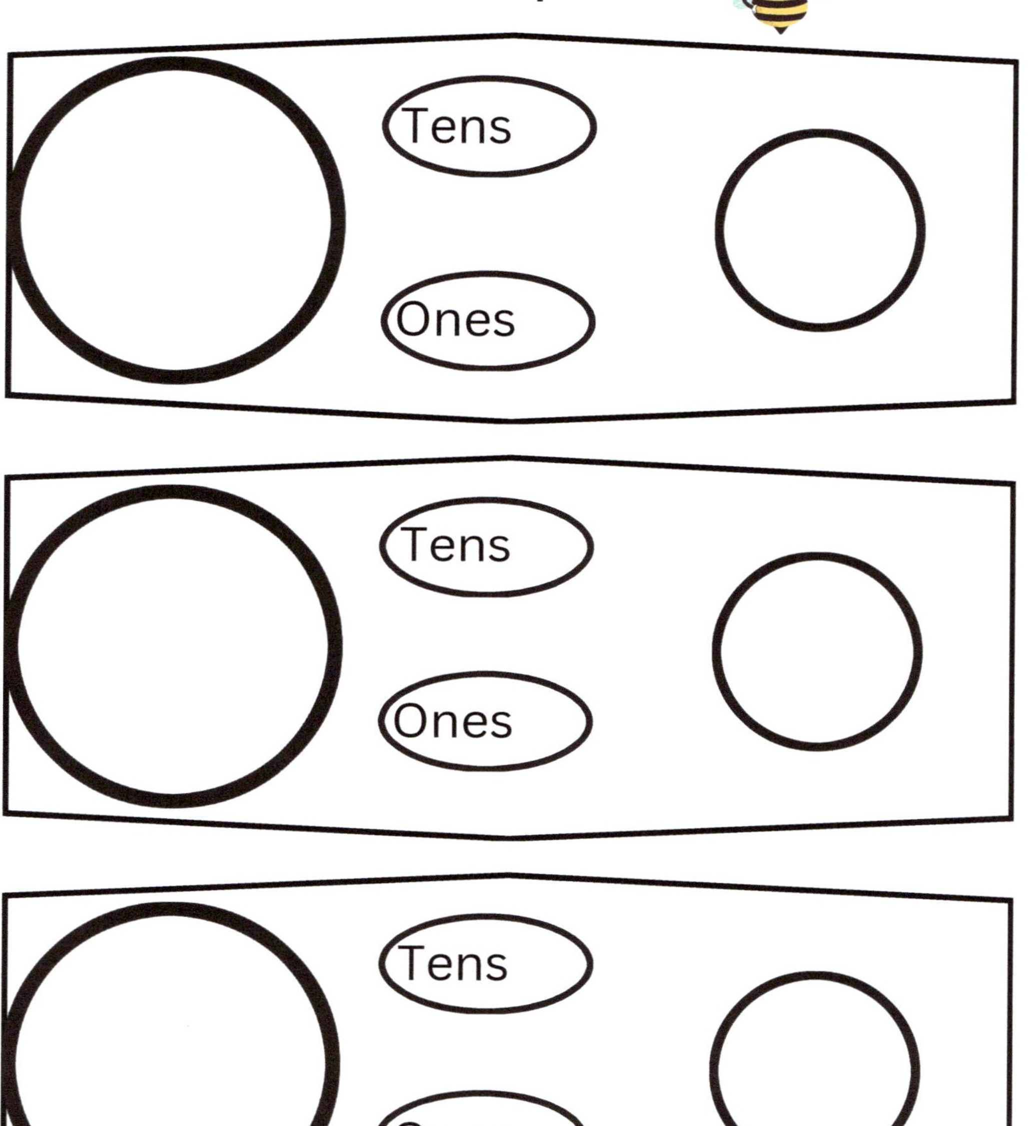

Place Value

7   18

Tens	Ones
	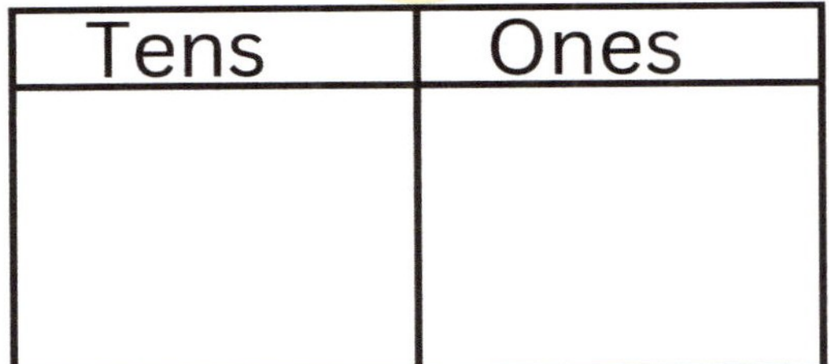

Tens	Ones

Tens	Ones

Tens	Ones
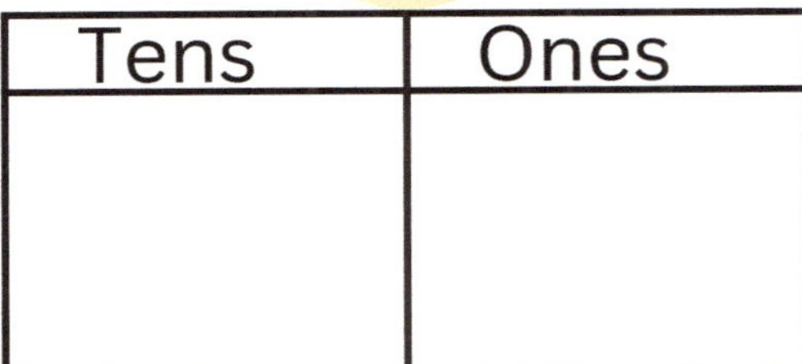	

Tens	Ones

Notes: These empty spaces are there for you to get creative with your little one!

C Brutus

This engaging educational book is designed to make learning mathematics enjoyable for children. It offers a variety of interactive activities that teach essential skills such as counting, addition, subtraction, and understanding number lines and place values and more. With its fun approach, this book encourages young learners to develop a strong foundation in math while fostering a love for numbers.

C Brutus

ISBN 979-8-3303-7369-7

9 798330 373697

90000